P.T.S.D.

Two

One Act Comedies

By

JONATHAN CHASE

Contact Information

Jonathan Chase, PO Box 90153, Raleigh NC 27675

CLSHP@aol.com

Dedicated to genuine humble political and economic reform worldwide

"Purloined" and "Cocktails"

ACT ONE

"Purloined"

"PURLOINED"

The play takes place in the morning at The Upside-Downside Diner in a fictitious southern city and state called "Either Way", "Purloined" in the United States.

The stage is set with two rows of banquettes and one row of stools at the counter.

The scene starts at a banquette

BETTY: Good morning, Rocky. You're late.

ROCKY: Top of the morning to yah, Betty. You can blame my tardiness on my P.T.S.D.

BETTY: What will it be today? The usual one-hour therapy session?

ROCKY: You got that right, plus two sunny sliders on the downside and grits.

People get up and leave and those waiting for a table are waved forward to take their a banquette

ACT ONE

BETTY: A booth has opened up. When was the last time we met, Rocky?

ROCKY: Under the bleachers at the football game, two weeks ago.

BETTY: Don't you wish.

ROCKY: Betty, you're in denial. Are your eggs on the menu today?

BETTY: Aren't you a corker. Let's keep it professional. If I recall correctly, we talked about your daughter's P.T.S.D and also a bit of yours. What did you say was the root cause of hers?

ROCKY: Spanish class.

BETTY: *Ahhh…Si!* You said, she didn't have a reliable source of mental healthcare services after Spanish class at the High School when in fact, I said, all she needed was a tutor.

ROCKY: It took her ages to find a therapist.

"PURLOINED"

BETTY: Wait a second. That fellah, he's scratching his ankles - exfoliating in our diner. Hey you! Stop that ankle scratching.

ROCKY: Can you put my order in? I'm running a bit late to Rebecca up from her therapist.

BETTY: How's your wife, Rocky? Is she still boxing you around?

ROCKY: We'll Betty, she is, as a matter of fact. I do appreciate you making the time to see her; and, that you're not charging her an arm and a leg, like you do me.

BETTY: As long as you buy breakfast here at The Upside-Downside Diner she's always welcome to talk to me for free. Both of us are boxers. But I think she needs drugs; so, she'll have to see a psychiatrist for those. I'm not licensed to give you anything for her but aspirin and your bill. Got that?

ROCKY: Got it.

The scene moves to another banquettes

ACT ONE

JUANITA: Welcome to The Upside-Downside Diner, my name is Juanita. I'll be your server today.

PAUL: Don't you remember me, Juanita? I was your immigration lawyer and got you the job here.

JUANITA: Oh sure, Paul. I do remember you. I was just pulling your leg. You were scratching your ankles.

PAUL: How's Purloined treating you? Let me introduce you to my wife, Jocelyn. She's new to the Upside-Downside Diner.

JOCELYN: Hello, Juanita.

JUANITA: You know, Jocelyn, my ancestors owned this whole state before yours stole it and renamed it Purloined.

JOCELYN: Really? How can you say my ancestors stole it when the land never moved? By the way, are you licensed?

JUANITA: Of course, I am. I own a Nissan.

"PURLOINED"

JOCELYN: No, hon, that's not what I meant. Are you licensed to give advice? Therapy that is? That's what I meant to say.

JUANITA: If you want your *huevos rancheros* without hot sauce then I am allowed to advise you to try the hot sauce and skip the *huevos rancheros*. How long will you be? I have a half an hour maximum limit to my therapy seasons, since I am a first year resident at the Upside-Downside Diner for all my P.T.S.D. cases. Are you trying to tell me that's what you both have?

PAUL: A half an hour will do, I guess. What do you think Jocelyn?

JOCELYN: I think that will do; sure, why not?

JUANITA: So, what's giving you both P.T.S.D? Paul, why don't you go first. Is your wife a boxer, too?

PAUL: Aren't they all?

ACT ONE

JOCELYN: *Paul!* Let's start with mine first. Juanita. I don't agree with our doctor's diagnosis.

JUANITA: What does the doctor say you have?

JOCELYN: She says we *both* have cancer.

JUANITA: Oh, I'm so sorry. What type of cancer?

JOCELYN: Tell her, Paul.

PAUL: She said we have cancer of the stars.

JUANITA: Of the stars? Ah, you both have nothing to worry about. She was just explaining that you're both born under the stars that make up birth sign of Cancer; or else, you're watching too many award shows. Not that you have any disease. Coffee?

JOCELYN: Hot tea for me.

"PURLOINED"

PAUL: Coffee for me, Juanita. We have some more issues, but we'll ask you about them later. I'm really hungry.

JUANITA: What do you want to order?

JOCELYN: "The Eggs-Purloined"...on the downside - easy for me.

JUANITA: And you, Jocelyn?

PAUL: I'll take "The Eggs-Either Way" on the downside. Stolen eggs? Really, Jocelyn? Did you have to?

JUANITA: *Blanchos Bandidos!*

JUANITA leaves to put in the order

The scene moves to another banquette

REGGIE: Delia, I wanted my eggs on the downside - scattered well.

ACT ONE

DELIA: Felix! Two eggs on the downside – scattered well. Order on the fly.

REGGIE: The fly? Margie, they feed flies here.

MARGIE looks over at another banquette

MARGIE: Just the mistakes, Reggie.

REGGIE: How can I trust the advice here is on the level if they mess up my order? What's your name, hon?

REGGIE Squints at her tag

Delia.

DELIA: Reggie, don't play games with me. Everyone knows everyone in Either Way, Purloined. Do you want me to play that recording you left on my phone?

REGGIE: No, don't do that.

DELIA: Margie, he's scrambling his eggs upstairs again.

"PURLOINED"

MARGIE: She's got you pegged, Reggie. She really does.

DELIA: How are you holding up with your P.T.S.D., Margie?

MARGIE: Are we still talking about Reggie, Delia?

DELIA: If you want to, we can.

MARGIE: No. Let's move on to another trigger, okay?

DELIA: Sure, how is your anxiety?

MARGIE: Our time isn't up, is it?

DELIA: *No-No!* Just relax - breathe.

MARGIE: I'm too anxious to talk about my anxiety, today. I want to talk about our dog. We think he has P.T.S.D. Tell her, Reggie.

REGGIE: We picked up Oopsie Poopsie from the vet and brought him home and all he's done since is sleep.

ACT ONE

MARGIE: We think he's depressed.

DELIA: Huh! Drugged or dead more likely. Don't you think he is getting over the medication that they must have given him?

REGGIE: He's been fast asleep for two days, Delia.

DELIA: I hate to be the one to bring this up, but don't you think Oopsie Poopsie may indeed be dead? Have you put a hand mirror to his nose?

REGGIE: Darn it. Margie, I told you to bring Oopsie Poopsie with us.

MARGIE: But they have a not pet policy at The Upside-Downside Diner.

REGGIE: This was an emergency, though.

MARGIE: Delia, we must go check on the dog. Cancel our order.

DELIA: The order is cancelled, but the charge still sticks!

"PURLOINED"

REGGIE and MARGIE drop money on the banquette and run out. Those waiting in line are waived in to take a seat.

The scene moves to the counter.

SYLVIA: Look, hon, I'm not going to tell you whether you should marry the guy or not, but dude (*pointing at the guy next to him*)...this guy your now talking to, calls himself Hazel, and has been coming to The Upside-Downside Diner since grade school dressed up as a girl. Run, don't walk, if you're seeking LGTB. This one is just a crossdresser.

Both diners get up; one hands SYLVIA some cash

SYLVIA: Keep the tip. That's from me to you both. Now go and accept yourselves with or without yourselves together. Who's next? Hey Truman and Lincoln! How *are* you both? Now here are two homosexuals, for sure.

The scene moves down the counter.

TRUMAN: Is Manuel available?

LINCOLN: Si! Is Manuel available?

ACT ONE

LINCOLN: Sure you do. Everyone has. If you love someone, you have religion. That's what I mean. Don't you love me?

SYLVIA: Did you vote, Lincoln?

LINCOLN: There wasn't even space for a write in, so I wrote in bold sharpie "MORSI" across the top of my classroom ballot.

TRUMAN: Is el-Sisi a homosexual?

SYLVIA: Who cares? What we should all care about is that 100% of the sentences carried out around the world, including in Egypt and Saudi Arabia, do not justify the severity of the crime – not even for murder.

TRUMAN: Yeah, I already knew that. I'm a lawyer. You read the ATLA newsletter we get it every month. That was in the column I wrote.

SYLVIA: I read it, too. Nice column. I'm an ATLA and Judge Judy fanatic.

"PURLOINED"

LINCOLN: Sylvia, can you ask Manuel where's my "Vice-Presidential"? It's so late that my name should be Truman by now.

SYLVIA: Speak for yourself, Myles Lincoln.

The scene moves to banquette.

ROSIE: Look, fellows, I told you all I know about it. You've been here an hour and a half and you've finished your meals and scratched your ankles way too much. If you're not going to have another breakfast or lunch, I can't give you another hour on my time without another one of your dimes. Rules are rules, so don't try to break'm under my nose. Apparently, you haven't been caught before until now.

Police officers enter the dinner and ROSIE waves them over.

Mike and Joe, these are the fellows you're looking for, I think. They've been flirting with the teller again, asking for more time on my dime.

ACT ONE

MIKE: Well, Rosie, technically that's not attempted robbery; that's just a bold request.

JOE: Mike's right, Rosie. There wasn't even a "Hands up!"

ALL stick their hands and arms up in the air.

MIKE: Hands down. We've checked their records. They're both clean.

ROSIE: But wasn't that solicitation?

JOE: Non-sexual solicitation is absolutely legal in Either Way, Purloined.

MIKE: Of course there are limits to the types solicitations allowed. You can solicit for breakfast, lunch, and dinner – even dessert. But, you can't solicit for unemployment; that would affect the numbers. Soliciting for employment is also prohibited. No soliciting allowed. You can put that sign in your window, if you want.

Diners get up and leave

The scene moves over to another banquette

"PURLOINED"

SYLVIA clears off the table.

SYLVIA: A booth is ready.

LINCOLN: I hate it when they say "booth" instead of banquette. Don't they know it was a bad break up between those two - a case of fatal P.T.S.D.

TRUMAN: You can't prove that, Lincoln. What do you think our P.T.S.D. will look like, if we break up?

LINCOLN: Whatever it will be, we'll come to the Upside-Downside Diner for therapy before we shoot each other. They really have the cheapest therapy under the Affordable Care Act.

The scene moves to the counter.

FELIX: Hi Francine. How are you doing today? Coffee?

FRANCINE: Please, Felix.

ACT ONE

FELIX: What's in your paper this morning?

FRANCINE: Hopefully, a non-sociopath looking to for an apartment to share. I'm suffering from P.T.S.D. since my last roommate left in a hurry two months ago.

FELIX: Let me guess. You're a boxer?

FRANCINE: Read his note.

FRANCINE passes FELIX the note

FELIX: "Gone fishing; be back later." You were rooming with a bee?

FRANCINE: He stung me, you could say.

FELIX: Have you Googled or Bing'd him in the police reports yet? Perhaps he's been arrested and wants to come back. Check the arrest records. You know, the coppers are still holding Occupy Movement leaders under tax evasion charges. All politically

"PURLOINED"

	motivated, so say the leaders. Was he one of those, you think?
FRANCINE:	I don't think so…So, you still think I should Google or Bing'm?
FELIX:	Of course, you should. Let me tell you what happened to a friend of mine. He broke into an empty house for sale to spend the night and ended up being arrested. After 24 hours, the coppers put him into a mental hospital without telling his next of kin. Patients have incredible rights to privacy; so much so, that you have a devil of time trying to find them once they get hospitalized.
FRANCINE:	So how did you find your friend?
FELIX:	I Googled and Bing'd him in the last town he was known to be in and presto, up popped the arrest charge. But it wasn't for squatting, though; it was for breaking and entering.
FRANCINE:	B & E? That sounds way harsh.
FELIX:	That's what I thought. What'll you have this morning?

ACT ONE

FRANCINE: Besides a new roommate, a bagel with an egg on top on the downside.

FELIX: "The B&E" it is on the downside, Francine. You got it.

FRANCINE: Thanks, Felix

The scene moves down the counter.

FELIX: Come on down, Free; a seat just opened up for you here at the counter.

FREE: Felix, I need your help.

FELIX: What's the word in high tech lately? How can I help you? Coffee?

FREE: Sure. It's not good. Not good at all. Our bottom line is on the downside, and our Director of Development has gone missing along with the surfboard that was hanging in the lobby.

FELIX: Do you think he took it?

FREE laughs

"PURLOINED"

FREE: Did he take it? Of course, he took it. He left a note that said, "Adios…Gone surfing". *Look!*

FREE hands him the note

FELIX: What's with all these notes? Why it could have been an inside joke. Gone surfing on the Internet, perhaps?

FREE: Not this guy. Look again. He signed it "Adios, Purloined! Back to Mexico."

FELIX: Yeah, he took the board alright. What was the fellow's name? I'll ask if anyone's seen a surfer. You can't miss somebody in these parts with a surfboard; we're landlocked.

FREE: His nickname is also "Free", just like mine. I gave him that name when I appointed him as our DOD, so that he wouldn't worry so much about our bottom line and on the downside.

FELIX: Any money missing other than in the daily operational costs?

ACT ONE

FREE: No, none whatsoever.

FELIX: You want my honest opinion, Free?

FREE : I do, Felix. I do.

FELIX: Hey, we're not getting engaged yet, *hombre*. But, let me tell you something. When an employee leaves a note saying "Adios" and takes your surfboard, he or she is not coming back until *le revolution!* In fact, most likely he has jumped a plane to Acapulco or gone to Stinson Beach to paddle out to the Farallon Islands where lies the Great White Diner. He's obviously an adrenalin junkie. You'll know it when the board shows up with a nice-sized chunky hole in it. Honestly, he must have just been tired of dealing with the sales aspect of his job; yearned for liberation in every sense of the word. You should look it this way. It's not your fault he left you to cook for us, here at the Upside-Downside Diner.

FREE: But I feel so guilty. *What!? Cooking for you!?*

FREE starts crying

"PURLOINED"

FELIX: Don't feel guilty. He's in a better place; making the pancakes just behind me. Get a better grip of yourself, Free. He loves his new job at the Upside-Downside Diner.

FREE: *Free!* I'm glad you're alive and happy, but where's my surfboard?

FELIX: Don't interrupt him; he's cooking. I'll tell you. Free got bored of surfing, so he gave it to me to pay off his P.T.S.D. and job-placement bill. He still isn't enrolled in the Affordable Care Act. And, I'm not listed as a provider yet; so, I'm now using it to learn paddle boarding.

The scene moves to a banquette

ROSIE gets on the phone.

MIKE: Rosie, can we finally get some menus over here? We're on a tight shift.

ROSIE: Hold you weapons, I'm on the phone with my day care provider. My kid has pre and post-traumatic stress disorder.

ACT ONE

JOE: Rosie sure has her hands full. I don't think she really has time for a full-time job.

ROSIE: Callie, what's up? Uh-huh? The kids are teasing your cats. Well, can you put your cats away? You can't?...Why not? ...You live in a studio... We'll, don't you have a door to your bathroom?...You can't put the cats in the bathroom?... Why not?...The litter box isn't in the bathroom... Well, where is it? The kitchen...Callie, that's just gross. How many cats to you have?...*Ten!?*

ROSIE yells

Will someone take Mike and Joe's order, I've got to pick up my kid from Callie's; cats have taken over her studio in the kingdom.

BETTY hands MIKE and JOE a couple of menus

BETTY: I got'm, Rosie. Don't you worry about a thing, except for those cats. You go on now. Can you pick up my kid, too?

ROSIE: Alright. I'll take them both to the other zoo.

"PURLOINED"

BETTY: Fine, but no reptiles or marsupials for Janel; they just gross her out.

ROSIE: Wait a second, I can't leave. I've got another therapy session with Victor coming up.

BETTY: What's his issue?

ROSIE: You know, already, Betty; he's bulimic.

BETTY: How many years has he been eating at the Upside-Downside Diner?

ROSIE: Oh, as long as I have been working here; going on thirty years - breakfast, lunch, and dinner; I don't cook.

BETTY: Are you still sleeping together, Rosie?

ROSIE: Of course not, he's my husband.

VICTOR enters.

BETTY: Here's Victor now.

ACT ONE

ROSIE: Victor, can you pick up Janel and the kid and take them to the zoo? The daycare sitter has lost control of her menagerie.

VICTOR: Can I get some breakfast first?

ROSIE: No you can't. You need to lose some weight. You're going to walk it off by take the girls to see the big cats.

VICTOR: Darn it, I've been out-boxed.

VICTOR leaves.

BETTY: What'll it be, Joe?

JOE: I'll take "The Eggs Either Way" on the downside and some more coffee.

BETTY: And you, Mike? What will you have?

MIKE: I'll take "The Purloined eggs" on the downside and a small orange juice.

BETTY: Any issues you fellows want to talk about? P.T.S.D. related, perhaps?

"PURLOINED"

MIKE: Oh, yeah. We see it all the time - domestic disturbance calls and all. I come home from work and the place is a mess, Betty. My kids are now calling the station since the house is so messy. Look, I'm a single parent with three youngsters. How do I handle that?

BETTY: I think you need to get a renovation at home, Mike; perhaps install separate jail cells for your three juvees, instead of having three bedrooms with no locks and each having their own cell phones.

MIKE: I never thought of that. Now there's an idea. They can play let's pretend. Who knows, by the time they're in middle school they should be scared onto the straight and narrow.

JOE: You hope.

MIKE: That I do.

BETTY: What about you, Joe? Any issues we should talk about?

JOE: We'll, I was in this firefight about a month ago and I saved someone's life. I don't feel like a hero because I had to take the hostage-taker out.

ACT ONE

BETTY: I understand how you feel. You aren't a hero; you've just been on a bad date.

JOE: Over my lifetime, I've killed – taken out - three.

BETTY: *Three*, Joe? I think you'd be better off if you came and cooked for us. Look, you guys have to stop taking people out.

MIKE: The only way to do that is to ban all handguns and assault rifles.

JOE: That will lower the amount of fatalities, for sure.

BETTY: All you have to do is talk some God-sense into the guy holding the hostage, then they'll free their captive. Here's some good news - an *Awake Magazine* for you both. Read it, before you think of killing someone again. Throw old time religion at them instead.

JOE: Okay, we'll give it a shot.

"PURLOINED"

MIKE: You could have picked a better word than "shot"?

JOE: What do you want me to do? Trade in one habit in for another?

BETTY: No, just try throwing your habit away.

MIKE: I'd be more awake if breakfast was already in my stomach.

MIKE: Joe, tell her about the other issue.

JOE: Which one? The're so many.

MIKE: The promotion.

JOE: Betty, the captain gave me a promotion since I rescued the hostage, but that means today is my last day of being on the beat with my partner here, Mike.

BETTY: Well, do you really need that promotion?

JOE: I'd like to have it, but I also don't want to leave my partner.

ACT ONE

BETTY: Can't you tell the captain that having your own squad car is not what you want?

JOE: He wouldn't understand, Betty. He'd think I was trying to run the station house, or something, behind his back.

BETTY: Well, is that what you really want to do?

MIKE: I think we would all like to be the top dog, but that's only wishful thinking for now.

BETTY: Take two aspirins, and think about it overnight. Then, come back here tomorrow morning. This is such a sensitive issue that I have to ask my therapist for her own opinion on how to handle it.

The scene moves back to the counter.

FELIX: A seat is open at the counter. Brian, come on down. My shingle is out, friend.

"PURLOINED"

BRIAN: Water this time, Felix.

FELIX: Coffee or orange juice is your co-pay. No water.

BRIAN: Orange juice then.

FELIX: Here's the menu. I'll give you some time. I know you're a slow reader. I could tell from your swagger that you're hurting and on the downside. What's up?

BRIAN: A copper shot me.

FELIX: That'll do it. Why did he shoot you?

BRIAN: I was in his way.

The scene moves to a banquette

JUANITA: Carlos and Gabriella, a booth is free.

LINCOLN: I wish this meal was free.

ACT ONE

CARLOS: ¿Hay un especial para el día?

GABRIELA: Sí, me gustaría que los huevos Benedict.

JUANITA: Café o naranja juie?

CARLOS: Café.

JUANITA: Any P.T.S.D. issues, you two?

GABRIELA: We do have some immigration issues still. But, for the most part, we are on the way towards the upside; so, it's only breakfast this morning.

CARLOS: Gabriela, let me talk to Juanita about our issue – the recently downside one.

GABRIELLA: *Carlos!*

CARLOS: We had a miscarriage about a month ago

"PURLOINED"

JUANITA: I'm so sorry for your loss.

CARLOS: It has really affected our relationship. Do you think we should try again?

JUANITA: Definitely try again. By the way, did you get your green cards yet from Paul?

CARLOS: They're still in the works. Can we come work for you until then?

JUANITA: I think we only have an opening for one at the moment, but let me check for you then let you know.

FELIX: "The I.N.S." order is up, Juanita.

JUANITA: Thanks, Felix. You work wonders.

FELIX: And two *huevos rancheros* orders are up.

JUANITA: Felix works miracles.

ACT ONE

FELIX: Give Manuel and Free all the credit.

The scene moves to a banquette.

DELIA: More coffee?

PAUL: Delia, tell Carlos and Gabriela not to worry about the I.N.S. It usually takes months to get a green card.

DELIA: What am I, your messenger?

JOCELYN: Can I have some more tea, Delia?

DELIA: (*Walking away*) Maybe.

PAUL: Delia has service issues.

JOCELYN: Did she also lose a son in the military?

The scene moves to the counter.

SYLVIA: More coffee, Truman?

"PURLOINED"

TRUMAN: Sure, Sylvia.

SYLVIA: Coffee, Lincoln?

LINCOLN: No, thank you…Sylvia, can I ask you a personal question?

SYLVIA: Sure, it's on your dime. No scratching of heels now.

LINCOLN: Are you compensated fairly here? Truman is a labor lawyer and he needs more labor. Any labor or employment related issues, you can count on him to help you out.

SYLVIA: Thanks, Lincoln. I will remember that if I need him in a future war.

DELIA: Who wouldn't? He's the one who dropped the atomic bomb. Our bathroom still hasn't recovered.

FELIX: Two orders up, Rosie: "Eggs Either Way" and "Eggs Purloined".

The scene moves to a banquette

ACT ONE

ROSIE: Thanks, Felix. Here you go Mike and Joe. Are you both awake yet?

JOE: I think I am. There's a lot of good material in here about compassion, but it may get me killed depending on the circumstance. If we can save more lives, I suppose it's worth it.

ROSIE: You bet it is. Remember, mental health is a community issue to be solved by all pulling together. We need our relatives safe and cared for as much as they need us.

The scene moves to another banquette.

DELIA: Reggie and Margie, your back! Another booth has opened up. I'll put your orders back in. How's Oopsie Poopsie?

MARGIE: He's still sleeping.

DELIA: You're both in denial. Just bury the dog. So what do you think of Mike's idea? Did you hear it?

REGGIE: What idea is that?

"PURLOINED"

DELIA: Banning all handguns and assault rifles.

REGGIE: I'd let law enforcement have them then force the officers to turn them all in on the day when they retire.

DELIA: I think one shotgun per household is more than enough for protection in Either Way. I am okay with that.

MARGIE: Yes, that way the N.R.A. can't say that the government has denied people their second amendment rights.

ROSIE: Not me. I'm with Mike. Ban them all.

DELIA: Sounds good to me, on second thought. Add a greater emphasis on mental healthcare services, free of change.

The scene moves to the counter

FELIX: *Delia!* Two eggs, two bacon strips, and hash browns on the downside – order up.

ACT ONE

DELIA: I didn't order that. Reggie, do you want it or should I give it to the fly? Just toast for you. Right, Margie?

REGGIE: I can take it.

MARGIE: That's right.

The scene moves to the counter.

TRUMAN: Check, please, Sylvia.

SILVYA: No more issues, boys?

LINCOLN: When are you going to start cooking on the upside at The Upside-Downside Diner?

SYLVIA: You'll just have to come by more often. Perhaps you just catch us every time on a downside day.

TRUMAN: Oh, I know we do.

"PURLOINED"

TRUMAN wipes the counter with his finger

TRUMAN: How's your cash flow?

SYLVIA: My name's not "Flow". Are you trying to rob me, Truman?

LINCOLN: Don't fret. I think it'll clear, Truman.

TRUMAN: That's not what the weatherman said this morning.

The scene moves down the counter.

FELIX: A counter seat has opened up. Who's the next victim?

ROBIN: It's you, Felix! *You!* How are you?

FELIX: A bit on the downside, Robin; a bit on the downside.

ROBIN: The cooking, too, I bet is as well. I got your phone message. Tell me more about your P.T.S.D. relapse.

ACT ONE

FELIX: Coffee or orange juice?

ROBIN: Water.

FELIX: No water. You can't just order water. You've got to have coffee or orange juice as your co-pay.

ROBIN: But I'm here to listen to *you* as *your* therapist.

FELIX: I can't afford your $100 deductibles. I'm going to listen to you and your P.T.S.D. issues, now that I have dropped you as my therapist on account of unaffordability. How do you feel about *that*?

ROBIN: Not good. I am glad you asked, though, because I feel a bit on the downside about it. As I look around here, I see a lot of my former patients like your deductible breakfast rates better than my flat fee under the Affordable Care Act.

"PURLOINED"

FELIX: We'll don't quit your day and evening jobs; that's all I can say. So how's being a comedian also working out?

ROBIN: The pay is better, being a comedian than a therapist. And, at least I get laughs rather than having to stock up on tissues. Last night, I opened up for a split end divorcee's meet-up group.

FELIX: Yeah, this economy really sucks. Most of us are working two to four jobs to pay our bills, depending if we're married and have kids. The Department of Labor, I'm sure, doesn't calculate that into their employment figures. If they do, they should be counting double. Major post-traumatic stress disorder sets in if you have two jobs over an extended period of time – like more than two weekends in a row.

ROBIN: So, who's treating your P.T.S.D. now?

FELIX: All I can tell you now is I am getting it all for free. Right, Free?

FREE: What's that, Felix?

ACT ONE

ROBIN: Felix, are you self-medicating again?

FELIX swats at a fly with a flyswatter

FELIX: Missed it. Ah, next time. So what will you have, Robin?

ROBIN: I'll take "The Downsider" with the eggs medium; two slices of wheat toast on the side; and, hash browns well scattered.

FELIX: Did you know that "The Downsider" is our favorite order on the menu?

ROBIN: I do now. Why isn't "The Upsider"?

FELIX: "The Upsider" eggs are served raw; just raw. If you have certain medical conditions, "The Upsider" can kill you.

ROBIN: Oh well, that explains it.

FELIX shows ROBIN a menu

FELIX: See the warning. Look, don't be so depressed, Robin. You knew that under the non-Affordable Care Act that

"PURLOINED"

                healthcare would still be unaffordable to the majority who still make close to minimum wage. It's all a sham. All heath care should be free. Right, Free?

FREE: That's right, Felix.

FELIX swats at another fly on the counter

FELIX: Missed it again. Free, let me have "The Downsider" with the eggs on the medium; two slices of wheat toast; and, hash browns well scattered.

ROBIN: All I can say is that the government is now stealing from the poor to give it back to the poor. It just doesn't make sense.

FELIX: Isn't that what you wanted, Robin? Sure it makes sense. The government has been stealing from us since the day it was created. The trick is to figure out a way for it to stop stealing from us.

ROBIN: What do you to do? Abolish money?

ACT ONE

FELIX: That's an excellent idea; else stop stealing. Right, Free?

FREE: That's right, Felix.

FELIX swats at a fly on the counter

FELIX: I finally got it. We have to abolish money!

ALL: *Abolish money!*

FELIX flicks the fly away with his finger

FELIX: Look, everything in the world is free for God's creatures, so why can't it be free for the rest of us humans? Free housing; free food; free healthcare; free education, etc. Free everything. *Awake! Awake! Awake!* To the good news (*yelling*) "You aren't free until everything is free!" Say it with me, everyone. "You aren't free until everything is free!"

ALL *You aren't free until everything is free!*

"PURLOINED"

FELIX: Right Free?

FREE: That's right, Felix.

FELIX: Now, we will still have to charge for breakfast until the government makes everything free. Being 19 trillion dollars in debt, we shouldn't have to wait too long for them to declare bankruptcy and for us to be truly free.

FREE: Order up, Felix. I'm going to home now.

FELIX: Why, Free?

FREE: It's where my second job is. I am a high tech finance consultant.

FELIX: Who do you work for?

FREE: The government.

FELIX: Which government?

FREE: I can't tell you.

ACT ONE

MIKE and JOE stand up and shoot FREE. Screams from the diners

FELIX: Oh my God, you've killed Free. *Now what are we going to do?*

FREE stands up

FREE: Don't worry, Felix; they shot me on purpose – with blanks. Just a birthday prank on you. Happy Birthday, old man.

FREE brings forth a birthday cake and ALL sing "Happy Birthday" to FELIX

ALL: Happy Birthday to you!
Happy Birthday to you!
Happy Birthday to you, dear Felix.
Happy Birthday to you!

THE PRESIDENT and VICE-PRESIDENT walk in with THE SECRET SERVICE

ROSIE: Ah heck, guess who just walked in visiting town. It's the president and vice-president.

ROSIE yells out

"PURLOINED"

Mr. President and Mr. Vice-President, It'll be a two months from Sunday wait for your mental evaluations at this V.A. hospital; so, you'd better take your cases elsewhere for speedier service - same to all you fellows in The Secret Service.

THE PRESIDENT, VICE-PRESIDENT, and THE SECRET SERVICE walk out

ROSIE: We have a booth available for the next customer. Oh my God, you must be really hurting. You're both bawling your eyes out. What happened, dearies?

EARL: I've been demoted to Double-A ball, Rosie.

ROSIE: Ah, don't worry about it, Earl and Laurie. My nephew, Phil, got called up from Double-A ball to play in the majors; so, not all is lost. It's a numbers game, Earl, as you know. Are you a pitcher or a fielder?

LAURIE: He's both, Rosie.

ROSIE: Multi-tasker, eh? Well, that's good to know and a strong selling point. What

ACT ONE

	you have to do is learn how to throw eight strikeouts in a game – minimum - and for the love of God, country, the game, and apple pie learn how to bunt, and bunt well. Got it. *Bunt!* Tell'm you can bunt like you can punt during football season.
EARL:	Rosie, you're an angel.
ROSIE:	I could be worse, I suppose. Now what will you both have to drink? Coffee or orange juice?
EARL:	Can I get both?
LAURIE:	Me, too?
ROSIE:	Hey, Felix, we have a couple of twofers. Two coffees and two orange juicers. That doesn't happen too often. Boy, that's a tongue twister. Say, it's pretty dark outside. What's that outside flying by? Felix, turn up the volume on the TV.

"Beep! Beep! Beep!" sound

TV:	Ladies and gentlemen we interrupt this broadcast with an emergency announcement. Residents living in the

"PURLOINED"

>Either Way area of Purloined take cover. A category four tornado has been spotted in your vicinity. Let me repeat, a category four tornado has been spotted in your vicinity. Take cover. This is a life threatening situation.

"Beep! Beep! Beep!" sound

DELIA: Everyone under the booths and counter!

Screams are heard from ALL

JUANITA: Don't worry, we'll have a post twister disorder workshop after it passes. Stay calm.

"Wooshes" are heard outside. Screams are heard from the ALL

ROSIE: I think it's passing.

DELIA: Who's passing?

ROSIE: Not who; the storm. Everyone stay calm. Mike and Joe, can you give us a heads up from the station on any areas impacted and which ones have been blocked off by emergency vehicles and personnel?

ACT ONE

MIKE: Okay, Captain Rosie. We'll give you a call. In the meanwhile, the safest thing to do is for you all is to stay put and wait for our update. Meanwhile, just watch the news.

JOE: You can eat, too.

The scene returns to the counter.
ROBIN: I'm also going to take my chances.

FELIX: Are you sure you want to leave, Robin. It looks really nasty out there. I wouldn't consider it safe to go out there until Mike and Joe call. You may encounter power lines and tree limbs blocking your way.

ROBIN: Felix, I should have brought my dog but you guys have a no pet policy. Bella has anxiety issues whenever she's left alone.

FELIX: Why, with a name like "Bella"?

ROBIN: She's seen herself in the mirror. She's scared of herself.

FELIX: Bella doesn't have anxiety, she has self-esteem issues.

"PURLOINED"

ROBIN: You really think so, Felix?

FELIX: I do. Lower the heat in the house, too. That'll help her cool down as well.

ROBIN: Felix, you were too hot?

The scene moves to a banquette

DELIA: Alright, everyone. By a show of hands, who still has anxiety about the twister? *All of you!?* What's the main concern?

CARLOS: Our families

ROBIN: Our pets.

FELIX: Our cars.

FREE: Our homes.

MARGIE: Our lives.

ROSIE: Let's talk about the last one, shall we? The chances of you being killed by a twister, even in Either Way, Purloined, are one in 60,000; so, it's a bit irrational

ACT ONE

to think that one of you has lost a family member or a pet because of it. There are only 20,000 that live in this town.

PAUL: What about some of us?

DELIA: Paul, you're being argumentative. The worse thing that could happen is that the wind blew your trailer over into the next town.

MARGIE: That's not funny, Delia. That's his retirement home.

FELIX: Margie, I wasn't intending to be funny; just being realistic. He should know that.

The phone rings

JUANITA answers the phone

JUANITA: The Upside-Downside Diner? Juanita speaking, how may I help you? Yeah, she's right here. Hold on. Rosie, it's for you.

ROSIE grabs the phone

"PURLOINED"

ROSIE: Rosie, speaking. Is this you Mike or Joe? No? Who is it then? Captain Fingers. So, Captain is there an update for us? Did I dis the president and vice president? How can you say that? I saved their lives. Think of it if they stayed in this town during that twister. They could have been two in 120,000 that dies in a twister. It was the best thing for them to get out of town. Best thing for us, too. I think they brought the the twister to town, anyway...I need therapy? God's will. It will be done. Is Mike or Joe there? No? I've got to go, now; I've got a workshop still going on post twister disorder.

ROSIE hangs up the phone and it rings once again

ROSIE: Upside-Downside Diner, Rosie speaking...Oh it's you, Mike. What's the word? Bad? How bad. Really? That many dead? Oh dear. Can you do a welfare check on Oopsie Poopsie? Let me know. Bye.

ROSIE hangs up the phone

DELIA: I guess the good Lord has brought many back together. God rest their souls.

ACT ONE

DELIA Crosses herself.

    Alright, let's all talk about how we feel.

ALL: We feel horrible.

DELIA: We all have to move forward. Forward.

ALL move forward a couple of steps and bunch up.

DELIA: That's not what I meant.

ROSIE: If we can live through horrendous U.S. foreign policy and the funding of dictators, we must get through this twister.

The scene moves to the counter

FELIX: To those still left standing, there's an open seat at the counter. Hi Pinky; so, what's the update from ground zero? Coffee?

PINKY: Chaos everywhere you look, Felix. Do you have any espresso?

"PURLOINED"

FELIX: What do you think The Upside-Downside Diner is? A coffee shop?

PINKY: No matter. Well, I felt like I was on an adrenalin rush just getting here to outrun that category four twister. Oh my God, wait till you see the damage and carnage on TV. I heard on the radio that Air Force One was flipped over on its side at the air force base with one of its wings shorn off in half. The president and vice president where quickly whisked to safety in a bunker just after it hit, having suffered minor scrapes and bruises. Marine One is on its way to pick them both up to bring them to Walter Reed for further evaluation.

ROSIE: Hopefully, they'll be involuntarily hospitalized.

FELIX checks his cell phone.

FELIX: The cell phones still work though; so the towers must still be standing. Imagine being without cell phone service for a minute. What will it be for you this morning, dear?

PINKY: What else? I'll take "The Twister" on the downside well; white toast; and, some grits.

ACT ONE

FELIX: You've got grit for just coming over here and ordering that. You'll be lucky if it doesn't kill you next time…Manuel, one "Twister" on the downside well; white toast; and, some grits. Any damage to your pink walls, Pinky?

PINKY: I can't say for sure. I high tailed it right here as soon as I heard it was coming - dodging debris thrown about along the way. Being a storm chaser is my second job. The stress of doing that is unbelievable. I remember driving through some Midwestern state in the middle of March and sure enough a twister was heading right towards me when I had all my belongings in a moving van and my car on the back of that on a tow. Goodness gracious, I was scared to death. You can't really outdrive a twister. You can just only pray and hope for the best that it misses you altogether.

"Beep! Beep! Beep!" sound

TV Ladies and gentlemen we interrupt this broadcast with an emergency announcement. Residents living in the Either Way area of Purloined take cover. A category four tornado has been spotted in your vicinity. Let me repeat, a category four tornado has been spotted in your vicinity. Take cover. This is a life threatening situation.

"PURLOINED"

"Beep! Beep! Beep!" sound

DELIA: Oh, no! Not again. Everyone under the booths and counter! On the double!

Wind and rain picks up and screams are heard from all

ROSIE: Remember one in 60,000! one in 60,000!

MARGIE gets up and looks into the parking lot

MARGIE: What about Oopsie Poopsie? Any news? Rosie, look at the parking lot!

ROSIE: Good God, definitely horrendous U.S. foreign policy. We're being attacked! We're being attacked!

FELIX: By whom, Rosie? Have they come to take Purloined back? By whom?

ROSIE: Not whom, Felix. By what! Hail, Felix. It's all hail in a hand-basket.

FELIX: Hell?

ACT ONE

CARLOS: ¡Dios mío! Diablos!

The scene moves to a banquette.

GABRIELLA: ¿es seguro salir?

JUANITA: Rosie, Gabriella asks if it's safe to come out.

ROSIE: Sure, but tell her not to go outside yet. It's still hailing cabs. God must be really pissed at those two men. What a legacy they've left: 42 million unemployed; the poverty rate shooting up to 15% from 12% when the president was first elected.

What happened to change and the prospect of guaranteed employment? Freedom from anxiety? Freedom from fear? And, freedom from ineptitude?

Felix, I'm going on break. I'm having an "All hail has broken loose attack". Manuel, make me an "Either Way" with wheat toast, and hash browns well. I'll take it behind the counter.

"PURLOINED"

FELIX: What are we going to do about this weather, Rosie?

ROSIE: Fix the foreign policy and you fix the weather. The two go hand in hand. Just you darn well believe they do.

FELIX: Why don't you become a diplomat or politician?

ROSIE: It's too late for me. We've made too many enemies. Besides, these men would never say they are sorry to all te people they've hurt; maimed; or, killed. They all have too much stubbornness to do the right thing. Tell you what, if two ladies do take over the highest offices in the land, then we will see some positive domestic and foreign policy changes; like removing all those boots on the ground from every country we've ever had a conflict with since this nation's first creation.

FELIX: Hey, I'm with you, Rosie. It's long overdue for women to occupy the top two positions. Their political slogan *should* be "We're not free until everything is free." And, their platform should include - mandatory free housing; free healthcare; free food; free

ACT ONE

                education; and, an end to homelessness and hunger all by the abolishment of money. The national debt created by all these men is enough in itself to show our ace hand - a pantsuit pair.

BETTY: I agree with you both. The country is the wrong footing and running on fumes. It's totally bankrupt. They're all in denial in Washington. We might as well stop printing worthless money when everything is going to be free soon anyway.

DELIA pours coffee

DELIA: Can you all visualize the day when the repo man finally comes to Washington? What a day that will be! Hah! I'll help them pack all those gaudy chandeliers, chairs, and every statue of every bigot and misogynist from our history right into the back of every truck.

FELIX: What shall we do with the chandeliers and chairs?

ALL: *Give them away!*

FELIX: What about the statues?

"PURLOINED"

ALL: *Throw them into the fire!*

DELIA: What about the Capitol and the White House!?

ROSIE points her right index finger and right arm upward in defiance.

ROSIE: *Let a woman decide!*

FELIX: That's Rollercoaster Rosie for you. Isn't she's the greatest?

FELIX bangs on a pan that sounds like a ringside bell

Rosie, you're "Either Way" is up!

– END OF ACT ONE –

ACT TWO

"Cocktails"

ACT TWO

The scene takes place in a prestigious hotel bar in Washington, D.C. The counter is placed on a diagonal with the actors facing the audience.

BARREL: Hello, Mr. Secretary, the usual today?

SHADOW: Sure enough, Barrel. Have you been following the news lately?

BARREL: Of course. The world is a mess, don't you think?

SHADOW: A mess, indeed.

BARREL: Do you think the North Koreans are up to it all?

SHADOW: I don't think so. Can your pour me a scotch and soda, please.

BARREL: But that's not your usual. What's up?

SHADOW: I need a little pick me up.

SHADOW looks around

"COCKTAILS"

SHADOW: I guess I'm the first one here. Can you arrange a special package for me again.

BARREL: It'll cost you.

SHADOW: Not the same. I need 1000 milligrams this time; so they say. I think it's overkill for the diagnosis, though. Perhaps I should tell the P.T.S.D. to rethink it. Yes, that's what I'll do. Barrel, I need to reserve the bar for an hour and a half. My daughter is going to get party with her sorority sisters. I need a safe place for them to do that. Can they do that here?

BARREL: I don't think the management will allow that. This is an upscale place.

SHADOW: Well, I got her into an upscale school.

BARREL: But, would you consider her an upscale girl?

PENELOPE enters wobbling.

ACT TWO

SHADOW: You be the judge. Here she comes now.

BARREL: Hi Penelope. Would you consider yourself and your friends to be upscale?

PENELOPE: What's upscale mean?

BARREL: Classy.

PENELOPE: Sure, we all go to class.

BARREL: There you have it, Mr. Secretary.

PENELOPE: Dad, aren't you going to offer me a drink?

SHADOW: I was hoping Barrel, here, would.

BARREL: No can do; for obvious reasons. She failed the sobriety test.

"COCKTAILS"

SHADOW: How did you get here, dear?

PENELOPE: I asked for directions from Ms. GPS.

SHADOW: She's studying cryptography.

BARREL: Impressive.

SHADOW: Tell the management we want it to be an open bar. If some of these students are carried back to their dorms by medics, they might study medicine someday.

BARREL: They'll certainly play doctor; that's for sure. If you can blow the Secretary's travel budget out of the water on an open bar at this hotel, why not try to get those knuckleheads to sign a Mideast peace deal.

SHADOW: I have tried and tried and tried.

BARREL: I heard about the Palestinians are going to the I.C.C. Good move, I'd say. Why on earth did you and Australia veto their induction to

ACT TWO

                      the United Nations as a full member?

SHADOW: We didn't want them to sit on the Security Council eventually.

BARREL: That's just outright prejudice.

SHADOW: You don't have to tell me that.

BARREL: Oh yes I do

SHADOW: Back to the original issue at hand. How much will the open bar cost?

BARREL: Don't worry. I think you can well afford it now. It's easy to figure out, anyway. Simply times the number of people by the number of drinks it takes to floor each, times the time of service – an hour and a half. How many classies are you expecting, Penelope?

PENELOPE: Hundreds

"COCKTAILS"

SHADOW: Honey, we'll talk about the party later. I'm expecting a good portion of the cabinet here any minute; so, go run along with Ms. GPS.

PENELOPE drinks up Shadows drink.

PENELOPE: Thanks, Mr. Secretary.

PENELOPE leaves wobbling

BARREL: Who are you expecting; the usual suspects? What about the vice president? Is he coming, too?

SHADOW: The vice president wasn't invited. Make it an open bar.

BARREL: You want to floor the cabinet? Can you pass out, too, so you won't be implicated?

SHADOW: Add it up for me.

BARREL: It comes to about $1000 if only a few of you show up.

ACT TWO

SHADOW: To the penny, please, Barrel.

BARREL gives SHADOW another drink

BARREL: $999.99. Now of course, if they order a fifth drink you're on the hook for that.

SHADOW: Alright, well you'll let me now if anyone tries to order a non-house drink that's over the average. I don't want to be left holding the tab for a $1000 glass of 19th century champagne.

BARREL: Done.

WHISKERS enters

WHISKERS: Hey Shadow? What's the word? Are there any peace agreements coming down the pike?

SHADOW: Those two are stubborn as mules, Whiskers. What's the word at HUD? Found any more money for Detroit? Honestly, that town looks like war zone – just like LaGuardia Airport.

WHISKERS: If you look closely at the budget you'll see where all the money is

"COCKTAILS"

	going to. It's not going into housing and urban development, but into the military industrial complex. We've got to talk with Metals about that. He needs to undergo massive layoffs in his war department.
SHADOW:	Give to Detroit what belongs to Detroit.
BARREL:	What will you have, Mr. Secretary?
WHISKERS:	I'll take a piña colada.
BARREL:	Mr. Secretary, that isn't a house drink.
WHISKERS:	So, are you trying to insult me because of my Latino heritage?
BARREL:	*No, Sir!* I am just trying to explain to the man who's paying the bill next to you that a piña colada is not a house drink and will cost $20. *He* wants to know.

ACT TWO

SHADOW: It's approved, Barrel. Go on, give it to him.

BARREL reads his cell phone

SHADOW: What are you doing, Barrel? You're supposed to be making Whiskers a drink.

BARREL: I'm contacting Ms. GPS to bring me some fruit. I need it to make the piña colada.

WHISKERS: Hey Shadow, I know about your deep disappointment with those guys over there in the Mideast. But look, there is a way around it that might prove helpful. In fact, there are many ways around it that might finally bring them to the table to make a deal.

SHADOW: I'm all ears. What do you do propose?

WHISKERS: Well, first there is the appropriations issue. We give them both a load of money –

SHADOW: We already do.

"COCKTAILS"

WHISKERS: What is it about four billion or so a year? Come on. And what do we get for that?

SHADOW: Their votes.

Messenger from Ms. GPS comes in with fruit delivery on his head.

WHISKERS: Okay, I see your point. Well then, what about more milligrams? Will appropriations support that; or, do we have to sidestep them again.

SHADOW: Whiskers, we're dealing with liberals and fundamentalists on both sides. How do you expect to get a peace deal signed when they don't agree amongst themselves?

WHISKERS: I see your point. We'll, perhaps you just support the liberal sides of both and that will end in the result you're looking for; which will, in theory, finally bring the fundamentalists back to the table for their signatures as well.

SHADOW: I think you're on to something there. The fundamentalist

ACT TWO

factions will never want to sign a peace deal if we remain convoluted. They're clearly not in the majority and are barely holding their own operating in a coalition; so, perhaps, we can get Ego to divide the coalitional governments on each side to turn the tables for us so that they'll all have to return to the peace table to sign a deal. We must work to give the liberals get the upper hand.

WHISKERS: Sounds good to me.

BARREL hands WHISKERS a piña colada

BARREL: Your piña colada, Mr. Secretary.

WHISKERS: Gracias.

EGO enters.

EGO: Sorry, I'm a little late. I had trouble finding a legal spot in which to park on K Street during rush hour. I had to use a garage.

WHISKERS: Which one did you use, Ego?

"COCKTAILS"

EGO: What difference does it make?

WHISKERS: Well, I wouldn't use the one owned by the Russians or Chinese. I used the one co-owned by the Emirates and Kuwaitis.

EGO: Which are the ones owned by the Russians and Chinese?

SHADOW: Let me see your parking ticket.

EGO shows SHADOW his ticket

SHADOW: Yup, that's the one owned by the Chinese.

EGO: How can you tell that?

WHISKERS: Let me see that.

SHADOW: It has a fortune on it.

WHISKERS reads the ticket

ACT TWO

WHISKERS: "Take the high road", it says.

EGO: I've been parking at that one before the days I joined the farm. They know everything by now.

SHADOW: Not very prosperous fortune ticket, if you ask me.

EGO: Who asked you?

SHADOW: No, he didn't.

WHISKERS: You'd better do a full sweep of it later for bugs.

EGO: I need a half-dozen drinks, Barrel; just water board me. Whisky sour – on the double – if you please.

BARREL: Mr. Secretary.

SHADOW: That's okay. Let him have it, Barrel.

"COCKTAILS"

BARREL: Okay, if you say so.

SHADOW: So Ego, Whiskers and I have this idea to break up the governmental coalitions in the Mideast in order to force a peace settlement. We want the moderates and liberals to win on both sides. Do you think you can help us out? Do you think your boys and girls can help destabilize the current governments – all at the same time so it doesn't look like one is trying to destabilize the other?

EGO: Has this operation been approved at the highest levels.

SHADOW: Come on Ego, you know not to ask that. Even if it was, we couldn't confirm it, either way.

BARREL hands EGO a whiskey sour

EGO: Do we have to kidnap anyone?

WHISKERS: Look, I don't want to be directly involved in the operational details. As long as they are all

ACT TWO

                    above board, I'm on board with my full support.

SHADOW: I approve of anything short of murder and torture for a peace deal.

WHISKERS: I'm tired of these folks, always claiming the limelight from blighted areas like Detroit which need our undivided attention. Detroit needs renewal, those guys need a rewind back 2,000 years or so.

EGO: You'll have no argument from me there. I certainly think they are acting rather silly. Let me look at the budget and let you know. I may need to borrow some funds from Metals.

SHADOW: How are the farmers holding up at the U.S. Embassy in Iraq? Are they getting enough of a rotation?

EGO: Well, I know 50% of ours are getting the rotation they need. Here comes the guy that you really need to ask.

"COCKTAILS"

METALS enters

WHISKERS: Metals. What the hell is going on in Iraq?

METALS: All hell is breaking loose, obviously. White Russian; hold the rocks, Barrel, if you please.

SHADOW: Do you think that it's time to clear out the embassy and put our boys on the battlefield again?

METALS I'm not sure that it's going to be enough. We've only got 5,000 troops in the embassy already and along with the Iraqi military they both can't seem to get past the ten yard line. To settle the place down, I think we would need about 100,000 more volunteers.

WHISKERS: *100,000?*

ACT TWO

METALS: That's right.

SHADOW: Heck, I don't think congress is going to go for that.

WHISKERS: I don't think so either.

METALS: So, it's going to be a long slog for a while. And, as far as the 5,000 are concerned, they are really there to protect the president of the country and his staff, in addition to the embassy which we've basically turned into one of the largest hotels and listening posts in the Mideast.

SHADOW: So what do you think about the Iraq plan?

METALS: What Iraq plan? We don't have an Iraq plan; we just have a ground commitment to a station till the end of time.

SHADOW: We can't simply leave a $750 million compound. We've got too equipment installed there; not to mention it's the only

"COCKTAILS"

	manufacturing base for our mechanics.
METALS:	Look, I don't think they're going to go in there guns blazing, knowing that.
WHISKERS:	Think Detroit. Do we really need more mechanics? I haven't seen the purchase orders to justify any more expansion at the embassy.
METALS:	Oh, it's going to be another mess. I am telling you guys. What about the collateral damage? How are we going to explain that? What on earth are we going to do if we nail a brigade of Quds forces? The Ayatollah is not going to be too pleased. It's a no win folks. Let's just stay out of the game as much as we can and let all the pieces fall where they may. This is *not* a containable situation from the air. We'll just have keep them from expanding beyond the two boarders.
WHISKERS:	I agree with you, Metals. It's a governing thing, too. These guys obviously don't know how to govern inclusively. That is why we are having all these problems.

ACT TWO

SHADOW: Well bombing them doesn't help either. Is the way to Basra cleared for the evacuation of staff, as far as you know?

METALS: No, we're trapped and surrounded.

EGO: Honestly, what kind of tactics did they teach you at West Point?

METALS: "Invasion Equals Surrender" was my favorite class. A scotch and soda, Barrel, if you please.

BARREL: Coming up. You know I served in Iraq - in Fallujah and Mosul. I tell you, I don't think these guys really ever got over Abu Ghraib. They are pissed as ever. And, I don't think there is anything you can do about it to appease them, except leave. They've got an agenda here and it's theirs to fulfill or not fulfill depending on the resistance they apply on the ground. Is it sectarian as well, sure; but, I think it's simply their form of impeachment and conviction for corruption and malfeasance of their own government leaders who have

"COCKTAILS"

                    climbed on your backs and sold their own people out.

SHADOW: Barrel, that's why I come here. Because I know I can always get sound and honest advice from you along with a well-made cocktail.

SHADOW drinks

WHISKERS: Barrel, I've got a question for you?

BARREL: What can I do for you, Mr. Secretary?

WHISKERS: Can you make me another piña colada, please?

BARREL looks at SHADOW

BARREL: Mr. Secretary?

SHADOW: Go ahead, Barrel. Unlike Ego, he doesn't drive himself either.

LIGHT BULB enters

ACT TWO

SHADOW: Hey, Light Bulb. Glad you could make it. Can you shed some light on the oil situation? Why is the price so low?

LIGHT BULB: The Saudis are flooding the market to destabilize the Russians who are supporting the Syrian government. It is as simple as that. The Jordanians put them up to it.

SHADOW: Can you prove that.

LIGHT BULB: It's about the refugee crisis that is spilling over into Jordan and Lebanon, too. Not to mention Turkey. They are all in on it. Gin and tonic for me, Barrel, if you please. The Jordanians are bleeding money and staples just taking care of these millions of refugees. It's a sad situation, but to blame it on the Russians is really beyond pale. It's our entire fault.

METALS: Let's not go into that. Barrel, doesn't have that type of clearance.

"COCKTAILS"

LIGHT BULB: Just shedding light on the situation.

EGO: That can get you sacked.

WELDER enters

WHISKERS: Afternoon, Welder. Just how do you intended to supply Baghdad, now.

WELDER: I still have some tricks left up my sleeve. We're going to do an air lift of supplies. That's right. No boots on the ground. Simply air lifts of needed supplies. We're going to load up a bunch of ospreys with barrels of oil and gas for the mechanics since the refinery was blown to pieces by mistake.

BARREL: Your usual, Mr. Secretary.

BARREL hands him a drink

Thanks, Barrel. So fellows, what do you think about the airdrop?

METALS: Gosh, I don't know since it puts more of our boys and girls on the

ACT TWO

                        front lines again. We might consider getting contractors to do the job.

EGO: Contractors would be cost-prohibitive.

SHADOW: Not a bad idea, Welder.

WELDER: So, is it a go.

ALL: It's a go.

WHISKERS: Let me check the FEMA inventory of temporary housing units – tents that is - we can drop on the Jordanians.

SHADOW: Make sure they get the drops right. Oil and gas to Iraq, and tents to Jordan.

WHISKERS takes out his phone.

WHISKERS: I'll text them.

"COCKTAILS"

LIGHT BULB: Expect 2 million more refugees if Baghdad comes under siege.

WHISKERS: Thanks for the shining light on that dismal prospect.

WELDER: Let me contact the air force to see how many planes we can line up. I think we should know where we stand in a couple of days.

SHADOW: That should be soon enough.

METALS: Haven't you been reading the papers. They are following the situation on the ground hour by hour, minute by minute; it's that fluid.

Phone rings at the bar and BARREL answers it.

BARREL: Yeah, he's here. Do you want to talk with him? Okay, here he is.

SHADOW: Shadow speaking...Really? Oh brother, I guess it's back to work. They can never seem to get their acts together accept on the battlefield against each other.

ACT TWO

Honest to God, I beginning to think that is what both of them were put on this earth to do – make misery for themselves and waste all of our time. Alright, thanks for the info.

SHADOW hands BARREL the phone

METALS: What's up shadow?

SHADOW: The Israelis and Palestinians are at each other's throats again. These limited cease-fires are almost as much of a nuisance as the conflict itself.

LIGHT BULB: Well, we've done the best we can to get them to the peace table.

SHADOW: We have another plan, Light Bulb.

Phone rings at the bar and BARREL answers it

BARREL: Yeah, he's here. Do you want to talk with him? Okay, here he is.

METALS: Metals here… Uh huh? Well that really surprises me, but I guess

"COCKTAILS"

                    we'll have to create more enemies since he wants it done. Alright, give them the go ahead on the plan we already discussed.

SHADOW: What's up, Metals?

METALS: We're surrendering. He's decided. Where going to create a whole bunch of more enemies – this time state-side – the majority in the House and Senate.

SHADOW: I think that's a given. But we already had made many enemies. There gets to a point where that is all your good at.

EGO: Bad foreign policy, Shadow. Blame it on that. That's what they say in Either Way, Purloined.

METALS: It seems to be a never ending viscous cycle, Ego. The U.S. and its allies dropping their ordinance all over the place and it only ends up in blowback and backlash.

WHISKERS: It's a calamity alright. Honestly, I am trying to think what I would do if I had the wherewithal to make

ACT TWO

	positive differences from afar other than just doing air drops. Ah, I have it. If I could, I would, go to cooking school; or, go on the show Chopped.
SHADOW:	Ditto. I love that show.
LIGHT BULB:	Another usual, Barrel.
SHADOW:	Why is peace so elusive, Barrel? Another drink, if you please.
BARREL:	Because you all covet thy neighbor's land and resources.
SHADOW: **LIGHT BULB:**	Two for two. Enough shop talk. It's a trigger for my P.T.S.D. Seen any good movies lately?
SHADOW:	No.
METALS:	*No?* I find that hard to believe, Shadow. You're always flying off to God knows where every other day for some conference or another; or, to try to put out some fire. Don't you have movies on

"COCKTAILS"

board that governmental jet of yours?

SHADOW: Are you kidding me? That's the only time I get some sleep. I can only sleep at high altitude.

EGO: Thank heaven you didn't choose to become a pilot as your profession.

SHADOW: Tell me, Barrel, you've been in some serious battles, obviously; you have a limp.

BARREL: I was born with that, Mr. Secretary.

SHADOW: How would you solve all the messes going around this world?

BARREL: They certainly can't be solved militarily, that's for sure. Too many children and innocent people are dying because of fools using indiscriminate weapons of mass destruction - taking out the innocents with cowardly joy sticks. It'll only take one country to get us started. Money has to

ACT TWO

be abolished. Everyone is paid in hours and has a forty-hour a week and forty-year work ethic who is able to work.

Homelessness and poverty is cured overnight. The country demilitarizes. And, we take care of each other in a humble way with luxurious accommodations in retirement and during hospice care.

The political, social, and economic fabric would be stitched with mighty humbleocracy thread; whereby the simple precept is that one is not free until everything is free; free housing; free food; free healthcare; free education; etc.

There is no reason why there should be haves and have nots around the word. We should all be haves and poverty should be finally abolished.

SHADOW: Barrel, sounds like the animal kingdom with laws; but, in reality, do you really think it can be accomplished.

BARREL: It's not a kingdom because there would be no kings. It would be perfect freedom under law.

"COCKTAILS"

METALS: Sounds like it would be put out of a job. Where'd you hear about Humbleocracy, Barrel? Is it your original idea?

BARREL: At a diner in Either Way, Purloined. From a lady named Rosie and her co-workers. You all could finally do something you always wanted to do without killing people or destroying things. Now, wouldn't that be a thrill?

EGO: I always wanted to clean toilets for free for a living, believe it or not. Perhaps they have an opening at the Upside-Downside Diner in Either Way for me.

BARREL: Cleaning toilets for living is certainly more honorable killing people; destroying things; and, air dropping from near and afar.

METALS: Barrel, we only do this because of worldwide corruption and heartlessness. Don't make us feel any guiltier than we already feel. After all, you're involved.

BARREL: Only so far. In a perfect world, and there is no reason why this

ACT TWO

shouldn't be a perfect world, we should all put our best efforts forward into Humbleocracy possible.

SHADOW: Is democracy out the window?

BARREL: Humbleocracy is a higher form of democracy; without all the heartlessness and built it deficiencies such as homelessness, poverty, hunger, injustice, and preventable diseases.

WHISKERS: You've got my vote, Barrel. I'm so disgusted with these politicians that I don't vote anymore. And, I used to be a politician.

METALS: So are you disgusted with yourself, too?

WHISKERS: I used to be, but not anymore since I have no accountability to any constituents, just to the president.

BARREL: But you're a secretary, so you must represent someone other

"COCKTAILS"

than the president. Since the president represents the people, you must represent the people as well. You take an oath to uphold the Constitution of the people, don't you?

SHADOW: I guess I represent the state and people of despair.

METALS: What is the national debt now?

LIGHT BULB: 19 trillion and counting.

BARREL: You're a point of light, Mr. Secretary.

SHADOW: We're so deep into the fiscal hole that we'll never get out of it.

BARREL: Unless humbleocracy is finally adopted.

EGO: Heck, I'm for it. As I say, I always want to clean toilets for a living for free.

Phone rings at the bar and BARREL answers it

ACT TWO

BARREL: Yeah, he's here. Do you want to talk with him? Okay, here he is.

METALS: Metals here... What do you mean you're not sure whether you hit the target? After you dropped a 500 pound bomb you should pretty well know whether you hit the target or not. Uh-huh? It was dusty. Well next time don't let Dusty drop the bombs.

METALS hands BARREL the phone.

Honestly, I should retire. I really don't feel too good about myself. I think I am going to hand in my resignation tomorrow. Iraq, Afghanistan, now back to Iraq again. Enough is enough, I think.

SHADOW: I'm with you Medals. If you do it, I will do it, too. What about you, Whiskers? *Whiskers!?*

WHISKERS: What's up? I was just catching up with the game. Still 0-0, bottom of the ninth.

METALS: Honestly, these players get paid millions and millions of dollars and they can't even get a hit or

"COCKTAILS"

                            bunt. Wait! Bags are loaded and Earl's up; he knows how to bunt.

LIGHT BULB: Perhaps, it's just great pitching. A double no-hitter in the works.

WHISKERS: You can't have a double no hitter, Light Bulb.

LIGHT BULB pulls out his phone.

LIGHT BULB: Sure you can. What if one team walks in a run? I think they just want to end the game early, so they all whiff. Besides, look at the stats of the pitchers on my phone. Both of them have ERAs in the high 3s.

SHADOW: There goes the bunt. Out at the plate. Way to go, Earl. Go Nats.

EGO: That didn't accomplish anything but create an out, Shadow.

SHADOW: I'm rooting for the Purloined team.

BARREL takes out a fly swatter and lets it down a swing on the bar.

ACT TWO

EGO: I'd feel better if they were earning Humbleocracy salaries.

SHADOW: Whiskers, about your resignation. Is it a go if I, Ego, Light Bulb, and Metals submit ours as well?

WHISKERS: Yeah, I guess I'll pull my tent, too. We've all retrieved our golden parachutes after our last drop, haven't we? I can't support any action the president and vice president are considering now. They are trying to stick their dirty little fingers into every jelly bean jar around the world. It's just not sanitary for them to do so.

EGO: Well said, Whiskers. Well, said - from the loo perspective.

SHADOW: I guess I'll have to learn how to get eight hours of sleep someplace else. Perhaps I will buy a hut on mountain top, perhaps in Nepal. I need the altitude for the right attitude.

METALS: Don't make it Mt. Washington? That would be too inside the beltway.

"COCKTAILS"

WHISKERS: Why not just adopt Barrel's philosophy and find a country that you think you can run on the Humbleocracy platform and win this time. Then, revamp the climate into a peace-loving humble society.

SHADOW: Do you think I can really do it, Whiskers?

WHISKERS: I wouldn't have suggested it if I didn't. Just make sure you have the right running mate this time.

SHADOW: You're right. I think I am going to go for it. I speak French, how about I try to run for president of France? I've been practically canvasing it every week on my way to and from the Middle East.

WHISKERS: Why not? I think it's a great idea. Go where the food and language is already second to none.

METALS: Barrel, how long do you think it will take Humbleocracy to be fully implemented in France, if Shadow wins the next election?

ACT TWO

BARREL: By directive, poverty, hunger, and homelessness will be eradicated overnight. Paper money would be abolished and the existing money could be recycled into toilet paper.

EGO: I like that idea.

BARREL: I thought you would.

WHISKERS: A toast to Humbleocracy!

ALL toast.

ALL: To Humbleocracy

SHADOW: How about all that free stuff? How does that work, Barrel.

BARREL: Each individual is issued an ATM card which would be act like a credit card. You can't just purchase 10 bottles of salad dressing for a family of three, unless you email the credit department that you're hosting a vegan garden party, for example.

"COCKTAILS"

LIGHT BULB: I think Humbleocracy is a brilliant idea. A toast to Rosie and her co-workers!

ALL raise their glasses.

ALL: *To Rosie and her co-workers!*

METALS: What about all those hoarders who use coupons to hoard massive quantities of toilet paper?

BARREL: When everything is free, you won't need coupons anymore. You will be limited on what you can buy within reason. Example: a family of four doesn't need 10 Cadillacs. We are going to combat greed and jealousy in any form that it is found. The purpose here is to make sure that no one goes without a need or justifiable want. Sound good?

SHADOW: Sounds perfect.

BARREL: One more thing. There will be term limits on every political and judicial position.

METALS: Now that is about time.

ACT TWO

LIGHT BULB: Of course term limits are about time. That's a no brainer.

BARREL: Any other questions?

SHADOW: How do we spread Humbleocracy to other nations from France?

EGO: Do we evangelize?

BARREL: We don't. That is how wars begin. The beauty of it is that we wait for the constituencies in other countries to demand it from their respective governments. Let it grow, just like flower power.

SHADOW: Barrel, have you always wanted to be a bartender? Is there any other profession you would rather be in? For example, would you consider being my campaign manager or running mate in France?

BARREL: Oh, sure; if you are serious about running on the Humbleocracy platform.

SHADOW: I am. We've got to change this world for the better – one country

"COCKTAILS"

at a time. So are you going to submit your resignation, too?

BARREL: I am, if you are ready to do this.

WHISKERS: When is the next French election?

SHADOW: Yes, when is the next election?

BARREL: About three years from now. But who needs an election. We need a peaceful humble revolution. About three months should give me enough time to brush up on my French.

METALS: Don't you have to be French citizens in order to run for the president of France?

BARREL: We are going to run on this platform and request world citizenship. The people will love it and support it. We won't believe in countrified borders. If any politicians try to block your eligibility, the people will not stand for it.

ACT TWO

METALS: You have a point. Shadow, I really don't think you can lose. The French are mostly populists. Scandals don't mean anything to them; so, as long as you're alive, I think you have a great chance at changing France and perhaps other countries if they see that Humbleocracy is really taking off there.

SHADOW: I am really pumped up about this new opportunity; or, else I am really drunk. Either way…

BARREL: Mr. Secretary, I would know if you were drunk. You're not drunk. You're just tipsy with excitement that perhaps, just perhaps, one of your peaceful endeavors is going to finally bear fruit.

EGO: We sure hope so.

METALS: What about you, Whiskers? Any plans for the future in France or otherwise.

WHISKERS: Oh sure. I'm a real foodie. I'd love to go to culinary school in France and become a great chef. What do you think?

"COCKTAILS"

LIGHT BULB: Perhaps you can make some great gourmet cat food.

BARREL: That's the beauty of Humbleocracy. It's not there to break any of your dreams. Education is free and as long as you are really suited to a profession based on your endeavors and hard work; and, sure, be anything you want to be, but remember you want to be at least good or great at it, so others can benefit from your expertise and talent.

WHISKERS: Got it. I'm so excited about it that I can hardly wait to pack my food taster – my cat, Wrinkles.

EGO: I'm also on board. I do have to talk to my wife and kids about it. They probably won't believe it until I actually move the dog dish.

SHADOW: Do you speak French, Ego?

EGO: I can learn from you.

ACT TWO

WHISKERS: Barrel, shouldn't Humbleocracy have its own language so that the whole globe can relate on a colloquial and literary level?

BARREL: Sure that would be perfect in a perfect world, but I think we can just invent an app that will do instantaneous colloquial translations. How about this? The nation that first institutes Humbleocracy is the first nation from which we adopt their language as the official language of humbleocracy.

ALL: *Oui!*

SHADOW: Who cares about any nation that tries to settle its problems by pumping up the military industrial complex anyway?

METALS: I sort of care. I haven't resigned yet.

SHADOW: Metals, you're not going to care after Humbleocracy is adopted because we are going to outlaw the military industrial complex worldwide.

"COCKTAILS"

WHISKERS: Let them eat fast food cat food for those that do care.

SHADOW: Don't worry, they'll get with the program, one day; especially when they start having a reverse immigration problems.

EGO: Wow! I didn't even think of that. How are we going to solve the immigration problem in France if everyone starts coming to France from around the world while other countries lag behind France in moving forward with progressive Humbleocracy.

SHADOW: Easy, we teach every immigrant a skill to return back to their countries with and give them everything for free. We sponsor them to then stay in their own country to advocate for Humbleocracy.

WHISKERS: Isn't that evangelizing?

SHADOW: No, that's poli-economic proseletyzing.

BARREL: Sure enough, we have to believe by the time they have finished

ACT TWO

their education they will have Humbleocracy to return to; or, they can simply stay in France. Most likely, they will return to their countries of origin once they are economically secure.

WHISKERS: Even to the United States?

METALS: I am not sure that will be the case in the United States. The U.S. has really stuck its foot in its mouth for decades, diplomatically and militarily speaking.

SHADOW: I suspect the U.S. will adopt humbleocracy in due time, but it won't happen until all the guns are handed into law enforcement. If that is done, then there is a chance for this country's future. If it isn't done, then there is no hope.

ALL Agreed.

Phone rings at the bar and BARREL answers it

"COCKTAILS"

BARREL: Yeah, he's here. Do you want to talk with him? Okay, here he is, Mr. President.

EGO: *Mr. President?* What does *he* want?

BARREL hands SHADOW the phone.

SHADOW: Shadow here. Ah, Mr. President. Where am I? I am at a bar with a couple of the other cabinet members. Ego, Light Bulb, Whiskers, and Metals. It's after hours, but what can I do for you? *Resign!?* Sure, but what about Whiskers and Metals and the others? Can they resign for you as well? Sure? Mr. President, you'll have our resignation letters on your desk first thing in the morning. But why may I ask? Because we dropped 2 million tents on Bagdad? Are you sure it wasn't Jordan. No? It was Baghdad. Is that so bad? It is? Why? The entire embassy staff retreated across the border to Saudi Arabia? Why did they do that? They thought they would have to sleep in vulnerable tents beyond the ten yard line? I see. Thank you, Mr. President, I can't thank you enough for giving us

ACT TWO

our freedom and this new opportunity. It's a blessing and an honor. Anything else? Humbleocracy is going in effect tomorrow? Really? And you're resigning as well? Mr. President, where did you hear about Humbleocracy? From the Upside-Downside Diner in Either Way, Purloined, too? Well, that's wonderful; just wonderful. What about all the guns in Purloined? Are they being confiscated, too? You're sending out the national guard tonight to confiscate them? Why I think that is a fine idea; just fine. Put it to them this way. Give up your guns, and get anything else – within limits – for free. They'll like that. What am I going to do? I am going to run for the president of France. Barrel, Whiskers, and Metals are going to help me win. You doubt that? Well, thank you for your unhealthy skepticism. You must be having a mean-spirited P.T.S.D. relapse. Good luck to you, too, in your new endeavors. What will they entail? You're going to convert jails into nails and dales. Sound positively messianic. If you do so, you'll have a chance at carving out some sort of positive legacy.

"COCKTAILS"

>Well, goodbye and good luck, Mr. President

SHADOW passes the phone to BARREL.

>Well you all hear that, we actually may have a free future to look forward to – hallelujah! Well, Barrel, what do you think of that?

BARREL: I'll believe it when I see that all the drinks on the house.

EGO: Let's celebrate with all the drinks on the house, Barrel. What do you say? Let's do it.

Phone rings at the bar and BARREL answers it

BARREL: Yeah, they're all here. Do you want to talk any of them? No? Okay, goodbye then.

BARREL hangs up the phone

EGO: Who was that?

BARREL: A colleague of sorts.

ACT TWO

WHISKERS: What do you say, Barrel? Drinks on the house, eh? It's time

FBI men and women run into the bar.

BARREL: It sure is. Here they come now.

FBI LADY: We're from the F.B.I. You're l under arrest for arms smuggling.

SHADOW: *Barrel?*

BARREL: Don't look at me, I'm just the informant.

SHADOW and the others are cuffed and being dragged away.

SHADOW: But who cares about the money and arms now? They're both being abolished! Humbleocracy is here! Humblecracy is here!

BARREL: It's about all your systemic corruption and glaring incompetence.

"COCKTAILS"

PENELOPE enters

PENELOPE: I just saw Daddy being thrown into the back of a tinted SUV. What's happening to him?

BARREL: He's being arrested.

PENELOPE: Don't they know he can't sleep at low altitudes?

BARREL: Perhaps they've all got a plane to catch. You know - rendition?

PENELOPE: Of what? I don't have a plane to catch, Barrel. How about a drink on the house? I've just heard the good news. Humbleocracy is finally here.

BARREL: Your usual?

PENELOPE: No, I'm no longer a monarchist since hearing the news. Bourbons are out and fundamental populists are in.

BARREL: Then what can I get you.

ACT TWO

PENELOPE: I'll take a "Red Russian with cranberry juice on the rocks.

BARREL: I think I will have bottled water. Let's toast everyone. *To the upside!*

All raise their glasses.

ALL: *To the upside!*

All drink up

BARREL: All it takes is a diner to change the world. Another toast! *To the diner!*

ALL: *To the diner!*

– END OF ACT TWO –

Printed in Great Britain
by Amazon